Mahatma Graces a Moneylender

Adapted from a Satsang story by

Sant Ram Singh Ji on January 10, 2016 & August 14, 2017

Illustrated by Carlos Brito

GO JOLLY
BOOKS

Mahatma Graces a Moneylender

Mahatma Graces a Moneylender is a story originally told in Satsangs by Sant Ram Singh Ji on January 10, 2016 & August 14, 2017 during Meditation Retreat Programs at RadhaSwami Ashram, Channasandra Village, Karnataka, India.

Special thanks to those who reviewed & critiqued the story:
some sevadars

Translated by Ashok Shinkar
Transcribed by Ali Czernin, Geoff Halstead, & Harvey Rosenberg

Carlos Brito has done a magnificent job illustrating this important book. He brings humor and beauty to the story through his unique style and viewers of his art love it! His magical illustrations dance off the pages and make adults and children see that there still is beauty in these difficult days. Thank you, dear Carlos.

ISBN-13: 978-1-942937-23-4

(c) 2017 All Rights Reserved

Published by
Go Jolly Books
www.gojollybooks.com
P.O. Box 2203, Port Angeles, WA 98362 USA

Mahatma Graces a Moneylender

Adapted from a Satsang story by

Sant Ram Singh Ji on January 10, 2016 & August 14, 2017

INTRODUCTION

Mahatma Graces a Moneylender shows the Limitless Grace a mahatma can bestow on an individual, even one who has done nothing good his whole life. A mahatma meets a moneylender and despite the fact that the moneylender has not done anything worthy of receiving the mahatma's Love, the mahatma gives his soul salvation.

Mahatma Graces a Moneylender is a beautiful story that demonstrates the great compassion, concern and love Sant Mat Masters have, not only for Their own disciples, but for the entire world. Even though the moneylender knew nothing of God and had hurt many people throughout his life, the mahatma chose to liberate his soul and free him from the clutches of Kal.

In January, 2014, at RadhaSwami Ashram, Channasandra Village, Karnataka, India, Sant Ram Singh Ji gave me permission to take stories He told in Satsang and publish them as books for children. He has allowed me to change His words directed to adults to words suitable for children. With His Limitless Grace, reviewers of the first ten books have told us children like the books.

Once again, Carlos Brito has given us joyous illustrations to accompany the words. His imaginative use of color coupled with his creative skills make whimsical characters and beautiful scenery. **Mahatma Graces a Moneylender** will impact children's and adult's understanding of our most beautiful Path and the compassionate Masters we are Blessed to have. We hope you enjoy it.

Radhaswami,
Harvey Rosenberg

Dedication

Sant Ram Singh Ji continues to shower His Limitless Grace making this book a work of art with deep meaning for Sant Mat initiates and seekers of truth. We are more appreciative and grateful than our words can ever express.

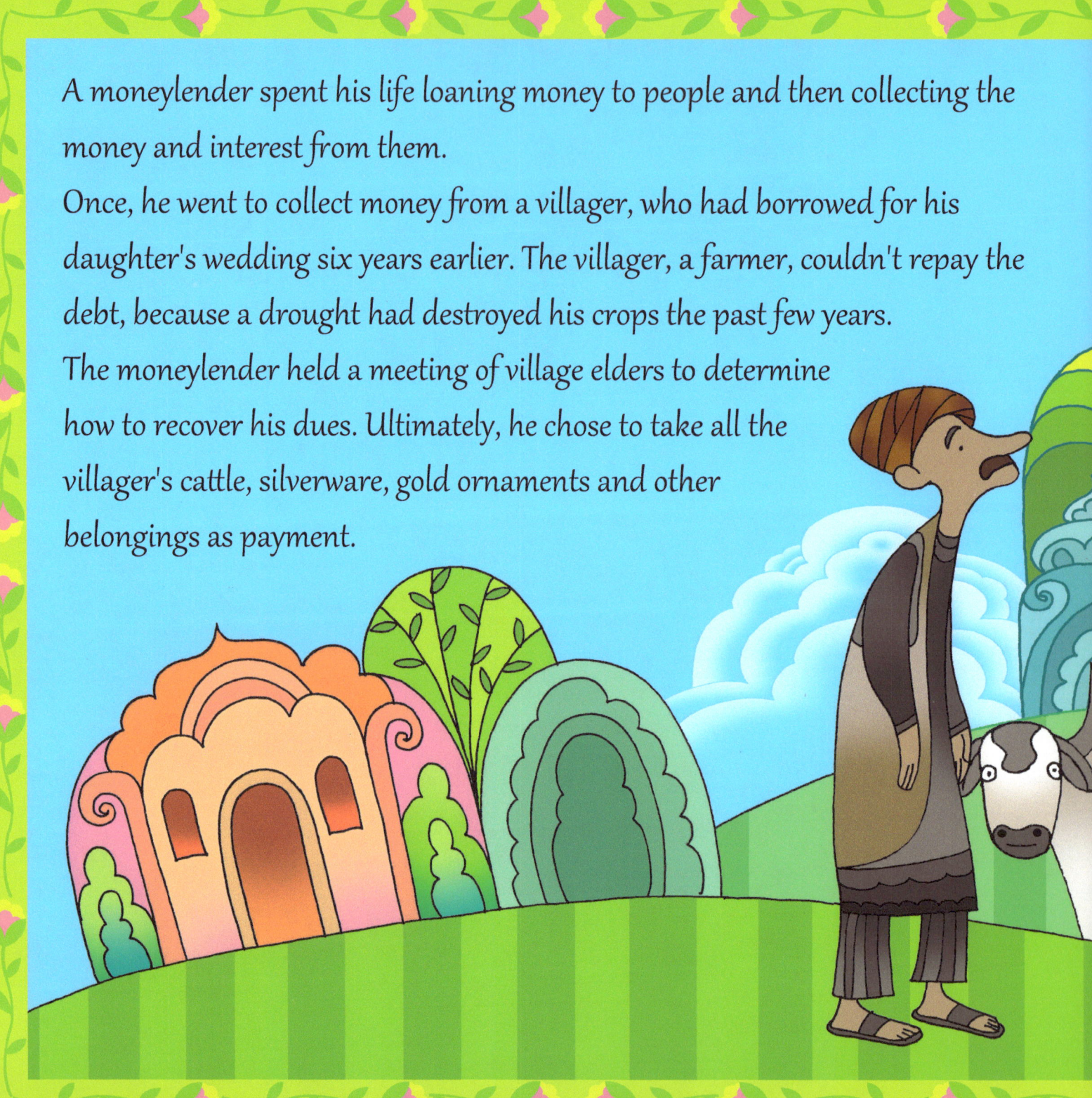

A moneylender spent his life loaning money to people and then collecting the money and interest from them.

Once, he went to collect money from a villager, who had borrowed for his daughter's wedding six years earlier. The villager, a farmer, couldn't repay the debt, because a drought had destroyed his crops the past few years.

The moneylender held a meeting of village elders to determine how to recover his dues. Ultimately, he chose to take all the villager's cattle, silverware, gold ornaments and other belongings as payment.

This upset the elders who said, "He is a poor villager. Please redeem some of his debt and interest. Let him keep some belongings."
But the moneylender would not do this and sold everything, which angered the villagers.

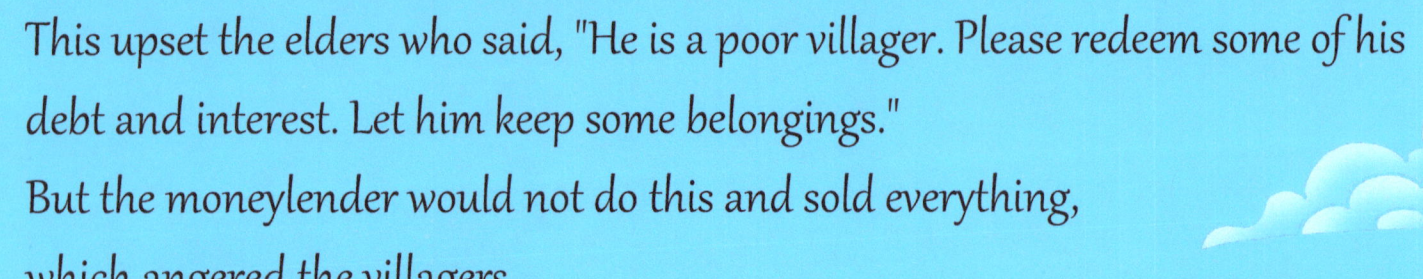

When the moneylender prepared to leave, he took his suitcases, bedding and all the belongings he traveled with. He stood at the side of road with his possessions, waiting for help in carrying them to the next village. But all villagers refused and because he was a miser, he wouldn't pay anyone to carry his stuff.

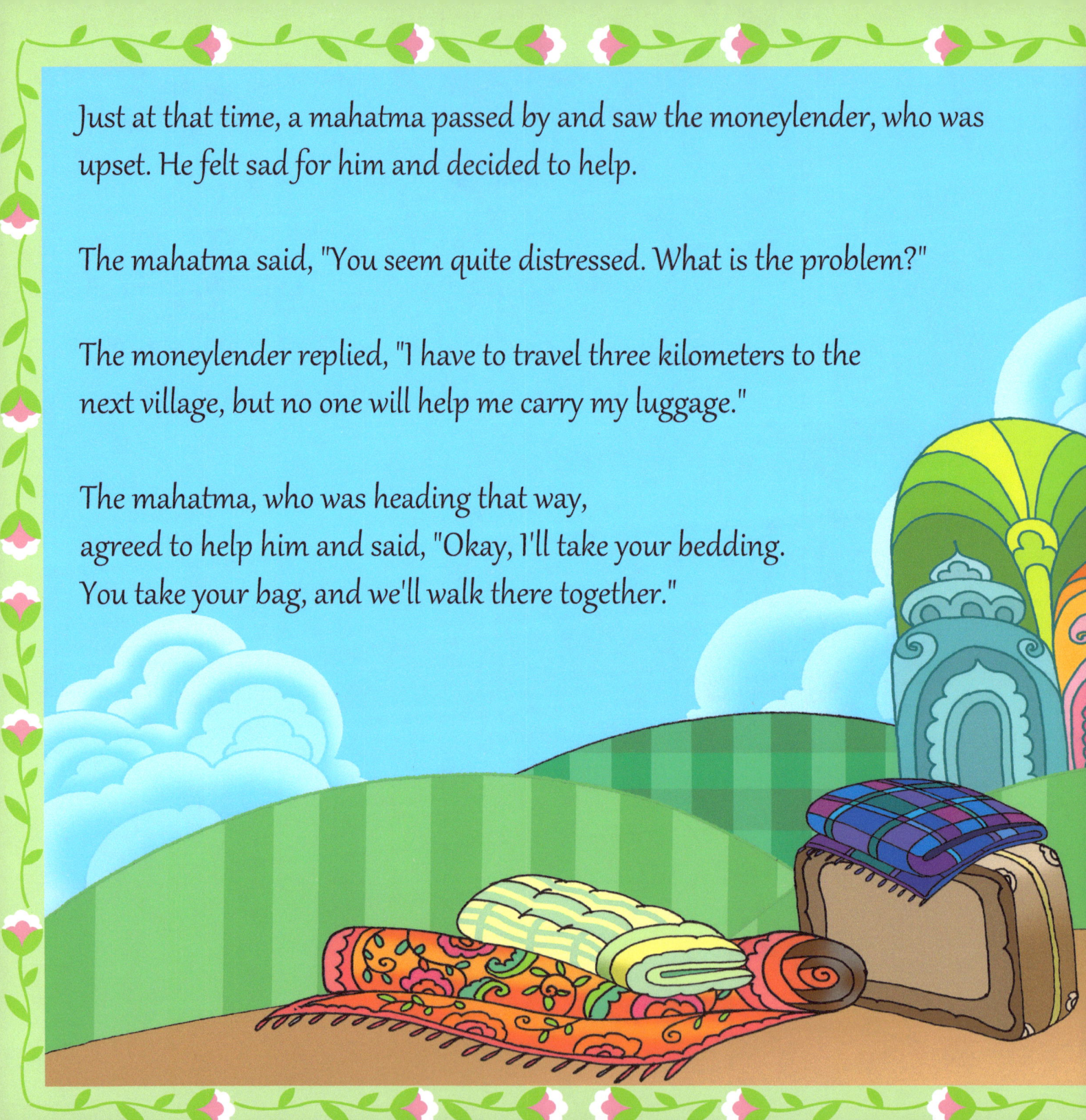

Just at that time, a mahatma passed by and saw the moneylender, who was upset. He felt sad for him and decided to help.

The mahatma said, "You seem quite distressed. What is the problem?"

The moneylender replied, "I have to travel three kilometers to the next village, but no one will help me carry my luggage."

The mahatma, who was heading that way, agreed to help him and said, "Okay, I'll take your bedding. You take your bag, and we'll walk there together."

When they started walking, the mahatma said to the moneylender, "I can't walk quietly. Either you talk about God Almighty and I will listen, or let me talk about God and you listen."

The moneylender said, "I've never listened to a Satsang in my life, so I know nothing about God. Why don't you talk, and I'll listen."

The mahatma then started talking about the importance of human life, the importance of devotion, about God Almighty, and spirituality.

After an hour, they reached their destination. The moneylender thanked the mahatma, and said, "Okay, leave the bedding near that tree and we can part ways now."

As they put the baggage down, the mahatma felt gracious toward that man. He felt that if he just walked away now, he wouldn't have fully helped him. Let me awaken him.

He told the moneylender, "Look, you have only eight days of life left. Whatever you want to do, do so in these eight days."

This frightened the moneylender. He immediately grabbed hold of the mahatma's feet and apologized, "I'm sorry for making you carry my bags. Please forgive me."

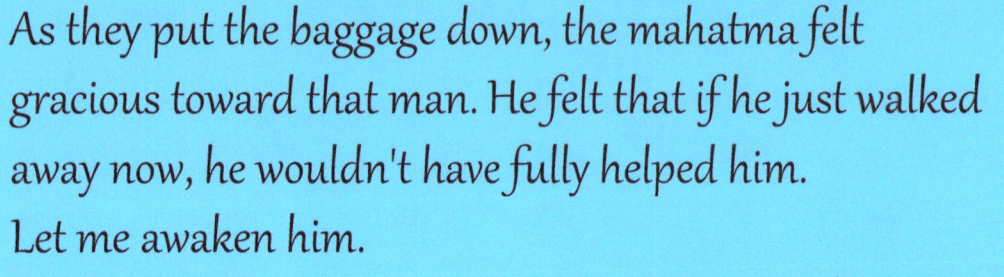

The mahatma replied, "It's not because I carried your luggage or anything to do with that. This was destined to happen. Since we spent one hour together, I thought I should make you aware of this."

The moneylender remained agitated, because he had lent so much money to so many people, and all that would be lost. In desperation, he prayed to the mahatma asking whether there was any possibility of being saved from death.

The mahatma said, "This situation cannot be changed. After eight days, the angels of death will definitely come."

But the mahatma wanted to shower more grace on him,
and further added, "It's inevitable that the angels of death will come,
and they will take you to the Lord of Judgment. He will look at your karmas.
He'll see that you have hurt a lot of people and the only good karma
you have is of that one hour we walked together. He will then ask you whether
you want to suffer all your bad deeds first, or first enjoy the
benefits of the one hour spent with me, and then suffer for all those bad sins."

The mahatma continued, "When he asks you this, say that you want the benefit of that good karma first. Then you will be asked, "How do you want to enjoy that good karma? Do you want to be sent to heaven? Or, do you have any other desire?"

When the Lord of Judgment asks this, refuse, and say, "I don't want to be sent to heaven or any other place. Send me to take the darshan of the mahatma with whom I spent the one hour of good karma."

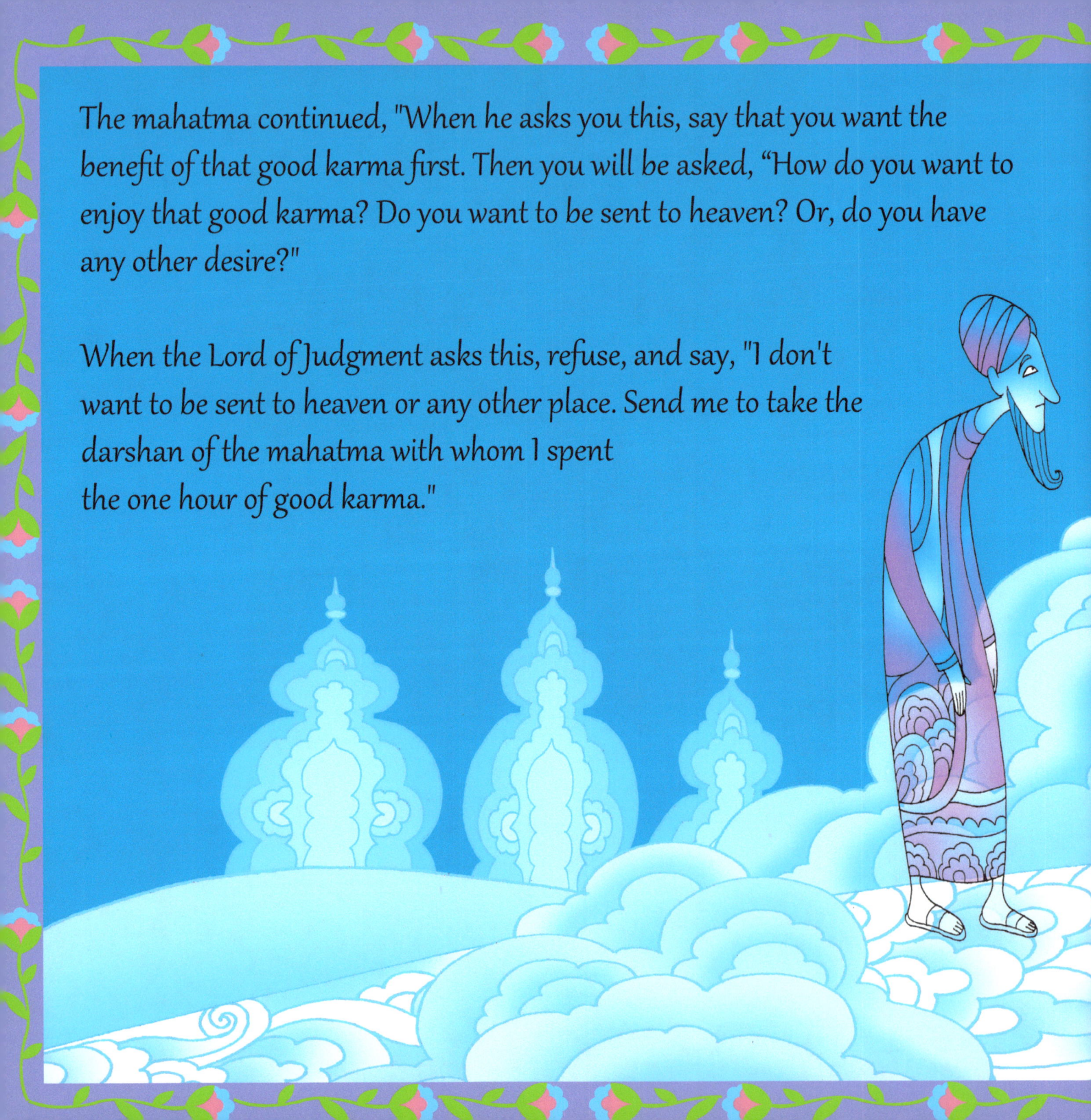

"Once you ask this, the Lord of Judgment must agree and his angels of death will bring you to me. This is the only solution you have. After that, I will see what to do."

In the first four days that followed, the moneylender transferred all his wealth to his son. Then, he spent the following days memorizing what he was going to say to the Lord of Judgment.

Accordingly, on the eighth day he died, and the angels of death took him to the Lord of Judgment. All his karmas were looked at. There was no good karma other than the time spent with that mahatma. Then, he was asked what he wanted first.
The moneylender replied, "My bad deeds are countless, it will take me a long time to settle those, so it's better that I take the one hour of good karma first. I want to go to that mahatma."
So, the Lord of Judgment called two angels of death, and said, "Take him to the ashram where that mahatma lives and allow him to be there for one hour. After that, get him and bring him back."

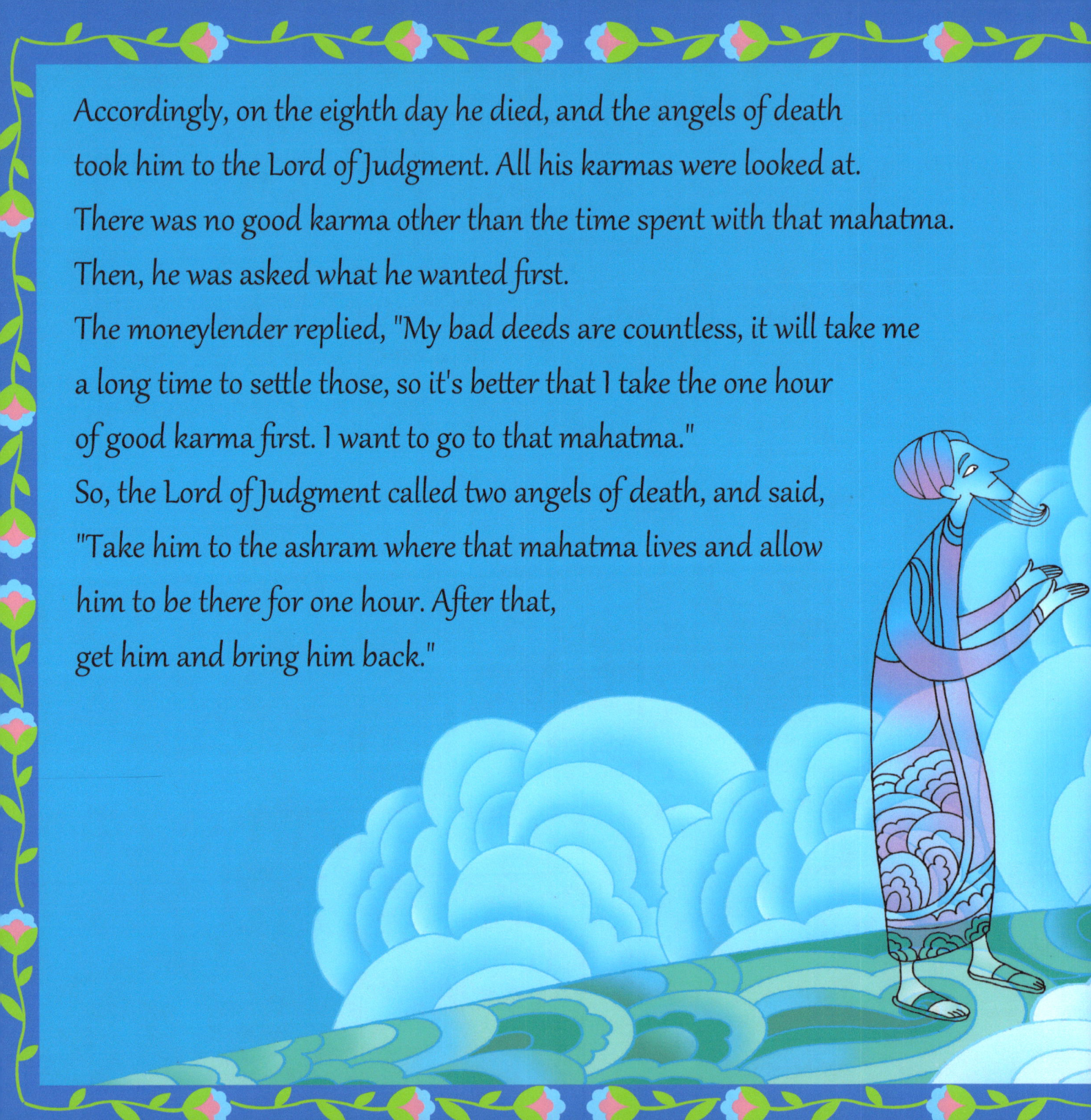

Once they reached the ashram, the angels told him to go in alone, because angels of death don't go where souls do meditation. They had to wait outside and said, "Come out after one hour."

When he entered the ashram, the mahatma recognized him. He said, "Oh, you've come."

The moneylender replied, "Yes, I've come. I followed your instructions."

The mahatma told him, "Okay, now, close your eyes and sit for meditation."

When the moneylender sat in meditation, he saw all of the things that had happened in his previous lives and was scared of those angels of death. He also remembered all the hells he had seen when he was with the Lord of Judgment.

He told the mahatma, "They're waiting for me and calling me to go outside."
"Time is up. Come out!"
The mahatma answered, "They will not come inside. They have to wait outside. Don't worry about them. Continue to meditate."
The moneylender listened to the mahatma and remained with him.
After a while, the angels of death left to inform the Lord of Judgment.

When the Lord of Judgment heard what had happened, he said, "He has gone into the protection of that mahatma, so we have no further role to play."

Mahatmas say that even if we spend just forty-five minutes of our lifetime in the company of a True Master, then millions of our earlier lives and the burden of all our karmas will end.

The mahatma's limitless grace took care of the moneylender by giving salvation to his soul.

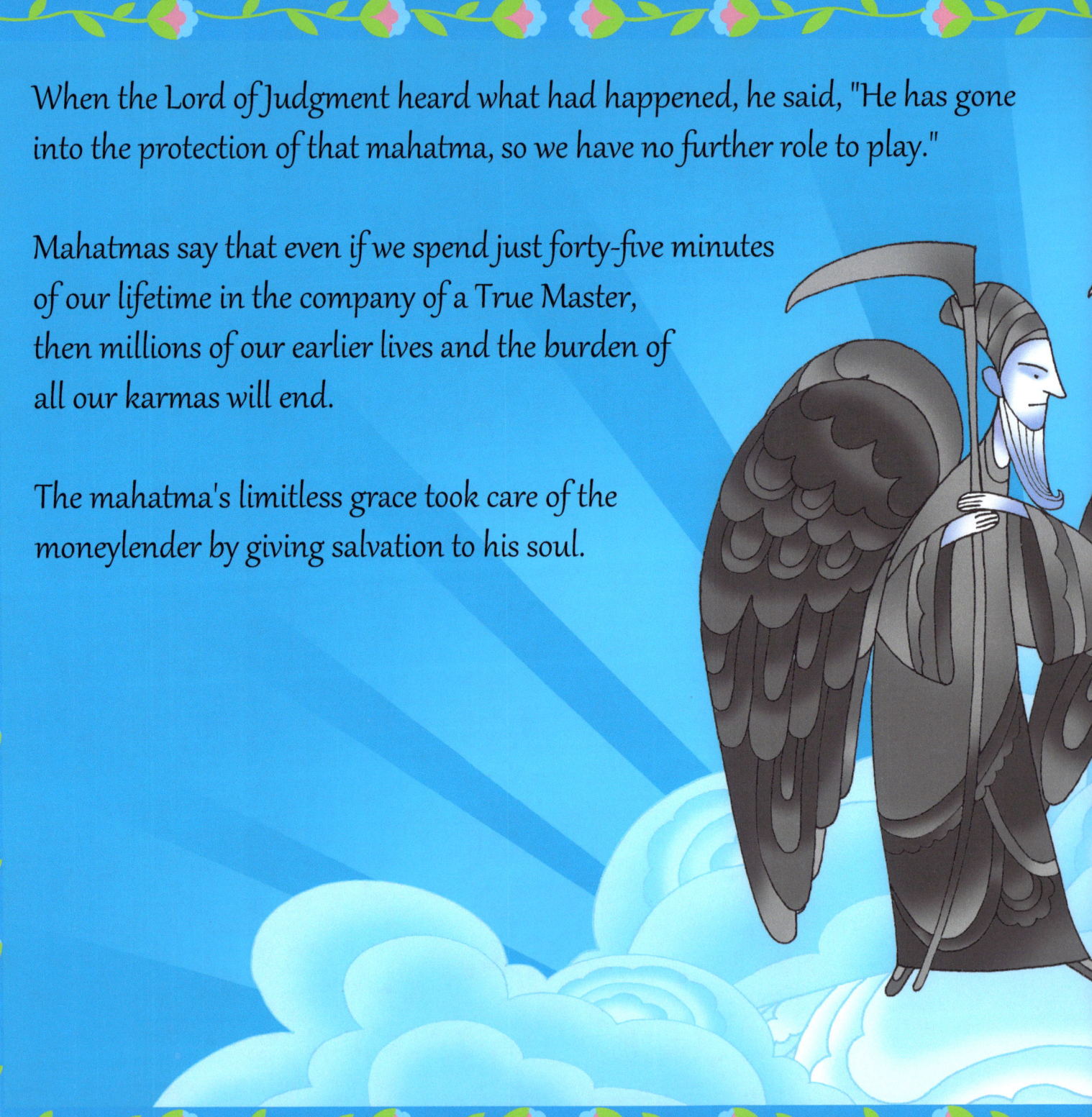